FAMILY COOKBOOK

Photography by Peter Barry
Designed by Helen Johnson
Edited by Jillian Stewart and Kate Cranshaw

4454

This edition published 1995 for Parragon Book Service Ltd.,
Unit 13-17, Avonbridge Trading Estate, Atlantic Road, Avonmouth,
Bristol BS11 9QD

ISBN 0-75250-696-X
Printed in Hong Kong

FAMILY COOKBOOK

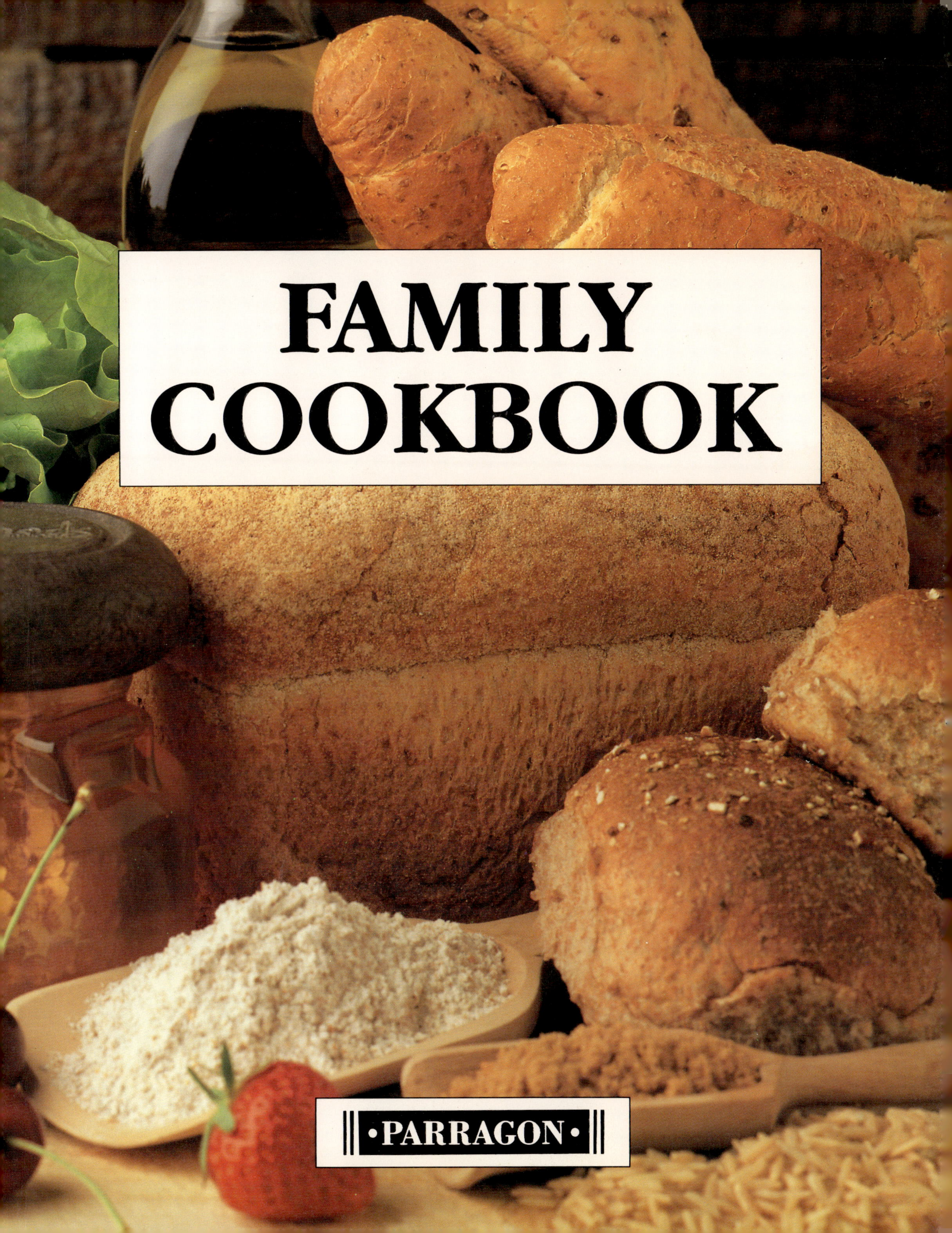

PARRAGON

Contents

Introduction

It's compliments not complaints that every cook strives for and none more so than those faced with feeding their family. But when time is tight and inspiration at a low ebb it is all too easy to resort to convenience foods or to serve that same old recipe again. However, last-minute dilemmas can be avoided by finding the time to plan a week's meals in advance, introducing some new recipes alongside the old favourites, and then drawing up a list of the required ingredients. Good planning also helps to ensure that a wide variety of foods will be offered each week, and in turn that each family member receives a good balance of the essential nutrients required for health. Each main meal should supply some form of protein, found in both animal and plant foods. Meat, fish, poultry and dairy foods all contain good quality or complete protein, whereas the vegetarian staples, dried pulses (beans, peas and lentils), cereal grains (rice, wheat, oats, barley, buckwheat, corn, millet), nuts and seeds contain smaller amounts of poorer quality or incomplete protein. When you want to eat a meal free of animal protein the problem of incomplete plant protein is easily remedied by serving the correct combination of plant proteins, for instance, rice and beans, beans and nuts, and leafy vegetables and cereals.

Consider also the amount of fruit and vegetables served at each meal. Experts now generally agree that each person needs five servings of fruit and vegetables (including fruit juice) a day. Fruit and vegetables are the main sources of vitamin C in the diet and supply other vital vitamins and minerals as well as being low in fat and a source of fibre. While increasing the amount of fruit and vegetables however, try to limit the amount of fat and sugar being used in cooking and at the table. Use butter, margarine, cooking oils and fats sparingly and try to discourage a sweet tooth by cutting down on sugary drinks, puddings and cakes.

Remembering to cater for individual tastes, it should be possible to base each main meal of the week around a different major ingredient i.e. meat, fish, poultry, eggs, cheese, pulses, pasta or rice. Take into account the style of recipe and method of cooking too. Introduce fashionable foreign dishes alongside more traditional recipes – stir-fries or spicy food one day, a casserole or pasta dish the next. Try serving a starter and a main course one day, a main course and a pudding the next.

Planning in advance for the week's meals also means that some preparation can be done in advance. Some recipes positively improve by being carefully chilled overnight, others can be prepared in advance then frozen, before being thawed out, reheated and served on the day. Ring the changes too by offering salads or finger foods in place of the usual sandwiches and rolls at lunchtime. After all, variety is the spice of life and also the key to successful family cooking.

SESAME CHICKEN WINGS

This is an economical starter that is also good as a cocktail snack or as a light meal with stir-fried vegetables.

SERVES 8

12 chicken wings
1 tbsp salted black beans
1 tbsp water
1 tbsp oil
2 cloves garlic, crushed
2 slices fresh ginger, cut into fine shreds
3 tbsps soy sauce
1½ tbsps dry sherry or rice wine
Large pinch black pepper
1 tbsp sesame seeds
Spring onions or coriander leaves to garnish

1. Cut off and discard the chicken wing tips. Cut between the joint to separate the wings into two pieces.

2. Crush the beans and add the water. Leave to stand.

3. Heat the oil in a wok and add the garlic and ginger. Stir briefly and add the chicken wings. Cook, stirring, until lightly browned, about 3 minutes. Add the soy sauce and wine and cook, stirring, about 30 seconds longer. Add the soaked black beans and pepper.

4. Cover the wok tightly and allow to simmer for about 8-10 minutes. Uncover and turn the heat to high. Continue cooking, stirring until the liquid is almost evaporated and the chicken wings are glazed with sauce.

5. Remove from the heat and sprinkle on sesame seeds. Stir to coat completely and serve. Garnish with spring onions or coriander if wished.

TIME: Preparation takes about 25 minutes, cooking takes about 13-14 minutes.

WATCHPOINT: Sesame seeds pop slightly as they cook.

COOK'S TIP: You can prepare the chicken wings ahead of time and reheat them. They are best reheated in the oven for about 5 minutes at 180°C/350°F/Gas Mark 4.

SERVING IDEAS: To garnish with spring onion brushes, trim the roots and green tops of spring onions and cut both ends into thin strips, leaving the middle intact. Place in ice water for several hours or overnight for the cut ends to curl up. Drain and use to garnish.

Parsnip and Carrot Soup

A delicious and wholesome country soup which makes use of that favourite vegetable, the humble parsnip.

SERVES 4

225g/8oz parsnips, peeled and sliced
225g/8oz carrots, peeled and sliced
280ml/½ pint vegetable stock
570ml/1 pint milk
Salt and freshly ground black pepper
Pinch ground nutmeg
1 small bunch chives, snipped
60ml/4 tbsps single cream

1. Cook the parsnips and carrots in the stock until tender – about 15 minutes.

2. Place in liquidiser or food processor, and purée until smooth. Return to the rinsed out pan.

3. Add the milk and season with salt, pepper and nutmeg, stir in the chives. Reheat gently to simmering point.

4. Stir in the cream just before serving.

TIME: Preparation takes about 10 minutes, cooking time is about 20 minutes.

PREPARATION: If a very smooth soup is required, the puréed soup can be strained through a metal sieve before the chives are added.

SERVING IDEA: Serve with crisp French bread and a vegetarian cheese.

FREEZING: This soup will freeze for up to 3 months if frozen before the final addition of the cream. This can be added just before serving.

Chicken Satay

This typical Indonesian dish is very spicy, and makes an excellent starter.

SERVES 4

2 tbsps soy sauce
2 tbsps sesame oil
2 tbsps lime juice
1 tsp ground cumin
1 tsp turmeric powder
2 tsps ground coriander
450g/1lb chicken breast, cut into 2.5cm/1-inch cubes
2 tbsps peanut oil
1 small onion, very finely chopped
1 tsp chilli powder
120g/4oz crunchy peanut butter
1 tsp brown sugar
Lime wedges and coriander leaves, for garnish

1. Put the soy sauce, sesame oil, lime juice, cumin, turmeric and coriander into a large bowl and mix well.

2. Add the cubed chicken to the soy sauce marinade and stir well to coat the meat evenly.

3. Cover with cling film and allow to stand in a refrigerator for at least 1 hour, but preferably overnight.

4. Drain the meat, reserving the marinade.

5. Thread the meat onto 4 large or 8 small kebab skewers and set aside.

6. Heat the peanut oil in a small saucepan and add the onion and chilli powder. Cook gently until the onion is slightly softened.

7. Stir the reserved marinade into the oil and onion mixture, along with the peanut butter and brown sugar. Heat gently, stirring constantly, until all the ingredients are well blended.

8. If the sauce is too thick, stir in 2-4 tbsps boiling water.

9. Arrange the skewers of meat on a grill pan and cook under a preheated moderate grill for 10-15 minutes. After the first 5 minutes of cooking, brush the skewered meat with a little of the peanut sauce to baste.

10. During the cooking time turn the meat frequently to cook it on all sides and prevent it browning.

11. Garnish the satay with the lime and coriander leaves, and serve the remaining sauce separately.

TIME: Preparation takes about 25 minutes plus at least 1 hour marinating, cooking takes about 15 minutes.

SERVING IDEAS: Serve with a mixed salad.

Garlic Mushrooms

An established favourite starter, this can also be served as a light snack.

SERVES 4

60g/2oz butter or olive oil
2 cloves garlic, crushed
¼ tsp chopped fresh thyme
¼ tsp chopped fresh parsley
¼ tsp chopped fresh sage
3 tbsps white wine
Salt and freshly ground black pepper
680g/1½lbs mushrooms, cleaned and quartered
8 slices of French bread
2 tbsps snipped chives
Fresh herb sprigs, to garnish

1. Heat the butter or oil in a frying pan and sauté the garlic until soft.

2. Stir in the herbs, wine, seasoning and mushrooms and cook over a low heat for 10 minutes or until the mushrooms are cooked, but not too soft.

3. Warm the bread in a low oven, if wished and serve the mushrooms piled onto the bread.

4. Sprinkle with chopped chives and garnish with sprigs of fresh herbs.

TIME: Preparation takes about 15 minutes, cooking takes about 15 minutes.

PREPARATION: This recipe can be prepared well in advance and reheated just before serving.

SERVING IDEA: Serve with sliced tomatoes.

VARIATION: Wild mushrooms are often available in good supermarkets; they make a delicious full flavoured variation to this recipe.

Spicy Prawn Wraps

Use large, uncooked deep-water prawns for this dish, look out for them in the freezer cabinet in Oriental shops.

SERVES 4

12 uncooked king prawns
1 clove garlic, crushed
1 stem lemon grass, soft core finely sliced
1 red chilli, seeded and chopped
1 tsp grated fresh root ginger
Juice of 1 lime
12 small spring roll wrappers
Oil, for deep-frying

1. Peel the prawns, removing their heads and body shells, but leaving the tail fins attached.

2. Remove the dark vein and 'butterfly' the prawns by cutting through the back of the prawns without cutting right through the bodies. Carefully open the prawns out.

3. Combine the garlic, lemon grass, chilli, ginger and lime juice in a shallow dish, and add the prawns.

4. Turn the prawns so that they are coated in the marinade, then allow to marinate in the refrigerator for 2 hours, turning occasionally.

5. Just before serving, remove the prawns from the marinade and wrap each prawn in a spring roll wrapper, leaving the tail end sticking out.

6. Heat the oil to 180°C/350°F in a wok and fry the prawn wraps in batches for 3-4 minutes or until golden. Drain on absorbent paper.

TIME: Preparation takes 20 minutes, plus 2 hours marinating. Cooking takes about 12 minutes.

COOK'S TIP: Keeping the tail fins on the prawns gives you something to hold on to when eating them.

BUYING GUIDE: Fresh or frozen spring roll wrappers can be bought in Oriental food stores.

Chicken or Turkey Pakoras

These delicious pakoras can be made with cooked as well as raw meat and it is therefore an excellent and unusual way to use left over Christmas turkey or Sunday roast. Raw chicken breast has been used for the recipe below, as it is more succulent than cooked meat.

SERVES 6-8

150ml/5 fl oz water
1 medium onion, coarsely chopped
2-3 cloves garlic, coarsely chopped
1-2 fresh green chillies, coarsely chopped; remove the seeds if you prefer a mild flavour
2 tbsps chopped coriander leaves
125g/5oz besan or gram flour (chick pea flour), sieved
1 tsp ground coriander
1 tsp ground cumin
½ tsp garam masala
½ tsp chilli powder
1 tsp salt or to taste
Pinch of bicarbonate of soda
340g/12oz fresh, boneless and skinless chicken or turkey breast
Oil for deep frying

1. Put 90ml/3 fl oz water from the specified amount into a liquidiser followed by the onion, garlic, green chillies and coriander leaves. Blend until smooth. Alternatively, process the ingredients in a food processor without the water.

2. In a large bowl, mix the besan, coriander, cumin, garam masala, chilli powder, salt and bicarbonate of soda.

3. Add the liquidised ingredients and mix thoroughly.

4. Add the remaining water and mix well to form a thick paste.

5. Cut the chicken into pieces and gently mix into the paste until the pieces are fully coated.

6. Heat the oil over medium heat; when hot, using a tablespoon, put in one piece of besan-coated chicken at a time until you have as many as the pan will hold in a single layer without overcrowding it. Make sure that each piece is fully coated with the paste.

7. Adjust heat to low and fry the pakoras for 10-15 minutes turning them over half way through. Remove the pakoras with a perforated spoon and drain on kitchen paper.

TIME: Preparation takes 20 minutes, cooking takes 30 minutes.

SERVING IDEAS: Serve with tomato chutney or the chutney of your choice.

Spring Rolls

One of the most popular Chinese hors d'oeuvres, these are delicious dipped in sweet-sour sauce or plum sauce.

MAKES 12

Wrappers

120g/4oz strong plain flour
1 egg, beaten
Cold water

Filling

225g/8oz pork, trimmed and finely shredded
120g/4oz prawns, peeled and chopped
4 spring onions, finely chopped
2 tsps chopped fresh ginger
120g/4oz Chinese leaves, shredded
100g/3½oz bean sprouts
1 tbsp light soy sauce
Dash sesame seed oil
1 egg, beaten

Oil for deep frying

1. To prepare the wrappers, sift the flour into a bowl and make a well in the centre. Add the beaten egg and about 1 tbsp cold water. Begin beating with a wooden spoon, gradually drawing in the flour from the outside to make a smooth dough. Add more water if necessary.

2. Knead the dough until it is elastic and pliable. Place in a covered bowl and chill for about 4 hours or overnight.

3. When ready to roll out, allow the dough to come back to room temperature. Flour a large work surface well and roll the dough out to about 5mm/¼-inch thick.

4. Cut the dough into 12 equal squares and then roll each piece into a larger square about 15cm/6 inches. The dough should be very thin. Cover with a damp cloth while preparing the filling.

5. Cook the pork in a little of the frying oil for about 2-3 minutes. Add the remaining filling ingredients, except the beaten egg, cook for a further 2-3 minutes and allow to cool.

6. Lay out the wrappers on a clean work surface with a point of each wrapper facing you. Brush the edges lightly with the beaten egg.

7. Divide the filling among all 12 wrappers, placing it just above the front point. Fold over the sides like an envelope.

8. Then fold over the nearest point until the filling is completely covered. Roll up as for a Swiss roll. Press all the edges to seal well.

9. Heat some oil in a wok to 190°C/375°F. Depending upon the size of the fryer, place in 2-4 spring rolls and fry until golden brown on both sides. The rolls will float to the surface when one side has browned and should be turned over. Drain thoroughly on kitchen paper and serve hot.

TIME: Preparation takes about 50 minutes for the wrapper dough, the filling and for rolling up. Dough must be allowed to rest for at least 4 hours before use. Cooking takes about 20 minutes.

Chicken Stuffed Peppers

Try a stuffing that is different from the usual meat and rice one for lighter tasting peppers.

SERVES 6

---

3 large green or red peppers
60g/2oz butter or margarine
1 small onion, finely chopped
1 stick celery, finely chopped
1 clove garlic, crushed
3 chicken breasts, skinned, boned and diced
2 tsps chopped parsley
Salt and pepper
½ loaf of stale bread, made into crumbs
1-2 eggs, beaten
6 tsps dry breadcrumbs

---

1. Cut the peppers in half lengthwise and remove the cores and seeds. Leave the stems attached, if wished.

2. Melt the butter in a frying pan and add the onion, celery, garlic and chicken. Cook over moderate heat until the vegetables are softened and the chicken is cooked. Add the parsley. Season with salt and pepper.

3. Stir in the stale breadcrumbs and add enough beaten egg to make the mixture hold together.

4. Spoon filling into each pepper half, mounding the top slightly. Place the peppers in a baking dish that holds them closely together.

5. Pour enough water around the peppers to come about 1.25cm/½ inch up their sides. Cover and bake in a pre-heated 180°C/350°F/Gas Mark 4 oven for about 45 minutes, or until the peppers are just tender.

6. Sprinkle each with the dried breadcrumbs and place under a preheated grill until golden brown.

TIME: Preparation takes about 30 minutes and cooking takes about 45-50 minutes.

VARIATIONS: Use spring onions in place of the small onion. Add chopped nuts or black olives to the filling, if wished.

SERVING IDEAS: Serve as a first course, either hot or cold, or as a light lunch or supper with a salad.

Spare Ribs in Chilli & Cream Sauce

Cocoa powder lends colour and depth to a sauce for ribs that's slightly more sophisticated than the usual barbecue sauce.

SERVES 4

1kg/2¼lbs pork spare ribs, in racks
1 tsp cocoa powder
1 tbsp flour
½ tsp cumin
½ tsp paprika
¼-½ tsp chilli powder
½ tsp dried oregano, crushed
Salt and pepper
225ml/8 fl oz warm water
2 tbsps liquid honey
2 tbsps double cream
Lime wedges and watercress, for garnish

1. Leave the ribs in whole slabs and roast in an oven preheated to 200°C/400°F/Gas Mark 6, for 20-25 minutes, or until well browned. Drain off all the excess fat.

2. Blend together the cocoa, flour, cumin, paprika, chilli powder, oregano, seasoning, water and honey and pour over the ribs. Lower the temperature to 180°C/350°F/Gas Mark 4 and cook the ribs for a further 30 minutes, until the sauce has reduced and the ribs are tender.

3. Cut the ribs into pieces and arrange on a serving dish.

4. Pour the cream into the sauce in the roasting tin and place over a moderate heat. Bring to the boil and pour over the ribs.

5. Garnish with lime wedges and watercress to serve.

TIME: Preparation takes about 20 minutes, cooking takes 50-55 minutes.

PREPARATION: Ribs may be cooked for the last 30 minutes on an outdoor barbecue grill.

SERVING IDEAS: Serve with rice and an avocado or tomato salad.

Crunchy Cod

Cod provides the perfect base for a crunchy, slightly spicy topping.

SERVES 4

4 even-sized cod fillets
Salt and pepper
90g/3oz butter, melted
90g/3oz dry breadcrumbs
1 tsp dry mustard
1 tsp finely chopped onion
Dash Worcestershire sauce and Tabasco
2 tbsps lemon juice
1 tbsp finely chopped parsley

1. Season the fish fillets with salt and pepper and place them on a grill pan. Brush with some of the butter and grill for about 5 minutes.

2. Combine the remaining butter with the breadcrumbs, mustard, onion, Worcestershire sauce, Tabasco, lemon juice and parsley.

3. Spoon the mixture carefully on top of each fish fillet, covering it completely. Press down lightly to pack the crumbs into place. Grill for a further 5-7 minutes, or until the top is lightly browned and the fish flakes.

TIME: Preparation takes about 15 minutes and cooking takes about 12 minutes.

PREPARATION: If wished, the fish may also be baked in the oven at 180°C/350°F/Gas Mark 4. Cover the fish with foil for the first 5 minutes of baking time, uncover and top with the breadcrumb mixture. Bake for a further 10-12 minutes.

VARIATIONS: The breadcrumb topping may be used on other fish such as haddock, halibut or sole.

Tandoori Chicken

The Tandoor, because of its fierce but even distribution of heat, enables meat to cook quickly, forming a light crust on the outside but leaving the inside moist and succulent.

It is possible to achieve perfectly satisfactory results by using a conventional gas or electric oven at the highest temperature setting, though the distinctive flavour of clay-cooked chicken will not be achieved.

SERVES 4-6

1.2kg/2½lbs chicken joints, legs or breast or a combination of the two
1 tsp salt or to taste
Juice of half a lemon
½-inch cube of root ginger, peeled and coarsely chopped
2-3 small cloves of garlic, peeled and coarsely chopped
1 fresh green chilli, coarsely chopped and seeded if a milder flavour is required
2 tbsps chopped coriander leaves
75g/3oz thick set natural yogurt
1 tsp ground coriander
½ tsp ground cumin
1 tsp garam masala
¼ tsp freshly ground black pepper
½ tsp Tandoori colour (available from Indian grocers in powder form), or a few drops of red food colouring mixed with 1 tbsp tomato purée

1. Remove skin from the chicken and cut each piece into two. With a sharp knife, make 2-3 slits in each piece. Rub salt and lemon juice into the chicken pieces and set aside for half an hour.

2. Meanwhile, put the ginger, garlic, green chillies, coriander leaves and the yogurt into a liquidiser and blend until smooth. Add the rest of the ingredients and blend again.

3. Pour and spread the marinade all over the chicken, especially into the slits. Cover the container with cling film and leave to marinate for 6-8 hours or overnight in the refrigerator.

4. Preheat oven to 240°C/475°F/Gas Mark 9. Line a roasting tin with aluminium foil (this will help to maintain the high level of heat required to cook the chicken) and arrange the chicken pieces in it. Place the roasting tin in the centre of the oven and bake for 25-30 minutes, turning the pieces over carefully as they brown and basting with juice in the roasting tin as well as any remaining marinade.

5. Remove from the oven, lift each piece with a pair of tongs and shake off any excess liquid.

TIME Preparation takes 20-25 minutes, cooking takes 25-30 minutes.

Beef in Oyster Sauce

You can make this spicy dish very quickly.

SERVES 4

460g/1lb sirloin steak
2 tbsps oil
¼ tsp ground cumin
¼ tsp ground coriander
175g/6oz baby corn cobs
120g/4oz can bamboo shoots, drained
175g/6oz mange tout peas
2 tbsps oyster sauce
2 tsps muscovado sugar
140ml/¼ pint beef stock
1 tsp cornflour
1 tbsp fish sauce

Garnish
Spring onion slices

1. Cut the beef into thin slices and then into strips.

2. Heat the oil in a wok and fry the beef over a high heat for 5 minutes or until cooked. Stir in the spices and cook for 1 minute.

3. Add the vegetables, then stir in the oyster sauce, sugar and stock, and bring to the boil.

4. Mix the cornflour with the fish sauce and stir into the pan, cooking until sauce thickens. Sprinkle with slices of spring onion to garnish.

TIME: Preparation takes 10 minutes and cooking takes 10 minutes.

COOK'S TIP: Partially freezing the beef will make it easier to cut. Slice into strips across the grain to keep the meat tender.

Stuffed Breast of Lamb

Breast of lamb is an inexpensive cut, which makes a good meal when boned, rolled and stuffed.

SERVES 4

Half breast of lamb
1 medium onion
Salt and pepper
120g/4oz white breadcrumbs
60g/2oz chopped suet
½ tsp marjoram
½ tsp thyme
Grated rind of half a lemon
Salt and pepper
1 egg
1 tbsp flour

1. Bone the breast of lamb with a sharp knife and trim off excess fat. Place the bones in a saucepan with half the onion and some salt and pepper. Cover them with water, bring to the boil, skim, cover the pot and simmer for 30 minutes.

2. Mix the breadcrumbs, suet, herbs, lemon rind, a little salt and pepper and the remaining onion, finely chopped, and bind them with the egg. Add 2-3 tbsps of the bone stock and spread the stuffing on the breast of lamb.

3. Roll up, starting at the wide end. Tie up firmly with string and place in a greased roasting tin. Bake in the oven, 200°C/400°F/ Gas Mark 6, for about 1 hour or until tender.

4. Transfer the meat to a serving dish and keep hot while you make the gravy. Drain off any excess fat from the roasting tin, retaining about 2 tbsps. Stir in the flour and heat until the mixture browns.

5. Stir in about 280ml/½ pint of the stock. Bring to the boil, stirring constantly. Boil for a few minutes and then strain into a gravy boat and serve with the stuffed lamb.

TIME: Preparation takes 15 minutes and cooking takes about 1 hour 40 minutes.

COOK'S TIP: Roast the lamb for about 20-25 minutes per 450g/1lb (including stuffing).

SERVING IDEAS: Serve with new potatoes and courgettes.

FIVE SPICE PORK

Serve this delicious, sweet, spicy dish with rice.

SERVES 4

675g/1½lb belly of pork strips
2 tbsps oil
1 tbsp curry paste
2 tbsps fish sauce
1 tbsp light soy sauce
2 tbsps sugar
1 tsp five spice powder
1 tbsp chopped fresh lemon grass (soft core only), or 1½ tsps dried

Fresh coriander and lime twists to garnish

1. Cut the pork strips into 4cm/1½-inch chunks.

2. Heat the oil in a wok and fry the curry paste for 2 minutes, stir in the fish sauce, soy sauce, sugar, five spice powder and lemon grass. Cook for a further 3 minutes.

3. Add the pork to the wok and cook, tossing frequently for 10 minutes until the pork is cooked.

4. Serve garnished with fresh coriander and lime twists.

TIME: Preparation takes 10 minutes and cooking takes 15 minutes.

PREPARATION: To prepare the fresh lemon grass, peel off the tough outside leaves and dry top portions, then chop the soft interior.

BUYING GUIDE: Fish sauce can be bought at Oriental stores and some supermarkets. If unavailable, mix together equal quantities of anchovy paste and light soy sauce.

Chicken Curry (Mild)

This mild curry is typical of northern India and has a lovely creamy sauce.

SERVES 4

1.4kg/3lbs chicken pieces
1 tbsp peanut oil
1 onion, finely chopped
2 cloves garlic, crushed
½ tsp grated ginger
2 tsps curry powder
½ tsp salt
1 tbsp vinegar
140ml/¼ pint coconut cream
140ml/¼ pint milk

1. Cut the chicken into smaller pieces: breast-meat into 4 pieces, thigh-meat into 2 pieces, and wings separated at joints.

2. Heat the oil until hot. Reduce the heat. Add the onion, garlic and ginger and cook gently, stirring continuously. Cook for 10 minutes, or until the onion is soft and golden brown.

3. Increase the heat and add the curry powder. Fry for 30 seconds. Add the salt and vinegar, and cook for 1 minute.

4. Add the chicken, and turn so that mixture coats the chicken well.

5. Add the coconut cream and milk, and simmer gently over a low heat for 20 minutes.

TIME: Preparation takes 10 minutes and cooking takes about 30 minutes.

SERVING IDEAS: Serve with Pilau Rice and poppadoms.

COOK'S TIP: Instant, powdered coconut milk can be used to replace the coconut cream and is a good item to keep in your store cupboard.

Macaroni and Blue Cheese

The classic combination of apples and blue cheese sets this delicious variation of macaroni cheese apart from its humble origins.

SERVES 4

340g/12oz wholemeal macaroni
Salt
90g/3oz butter
90g/3oz plain flour
570ml/1 pint milk
1 tsp dried or fresh chopped tarragon
225g/8oz vegetarian blue cheese, crumbled or grated
Freshly ground black pepper
2 tbsps vegetable oil
2 apples, cored and chopped
2 onions, chopped
1 clove garlic, crushed
Sprig of fresh tarragon, to garnish

1. Cook the macaroni in plenty of lightly salted boiling water for 12 minutes until 'al dente' or as directed on the packet. Drain well.

2. Meanwhile melt the butter in a saucepan, stir in the flour, and cook for 1 minute.

3. Remove from the heat and gradually stir in the milk. Return to the heat and bring to the boil, stirring constantly, then simmer for 1-2 minutes.

4. Stir in the tarragon and blue cheese and cook until the cheese melts, taste and season with salt if needed and freshly ground pepper.

5. In a smaller pan heat the oil and sauté the apple, onion and garlic for 5 minutes until just soft.

6. Mix the apple and onion into the sauce then stir in the drained pasta, return to the heat to warm through the pasta if necessary. Serve garnished with a sprig of fresh tarragon.

TIME: Preparation takes about 5 minutes, cooking takes about 20 minutes.

VARIATION: Use sage instead of the tarragon in this recipe.

Herb and Onion Grilled Lamb Chops

These chops are quick to prepare. The marinade gives them a lovely flavour and keeps the meat moist during cooking.

SERVES 4

4 leg chops, cut 2cm/¾-inch thick

Marinade
1 large onion, finely chopped
1 tbsp parsley, finely chopped
1 tbsp fresh thyme or mint leaves, roughly chopped
2 fresh bay leaves, bruised
1 clove garlic, crushed
3 tbsps oil
Juice of ½ lemon
Salt and pepper

1. Combine all the marinade ingredients and pour over the chops in a dish.

2. Cover and marinate for 2 hours in the refrigerator.

3. Place the chops on a rack over hot coals and cook for about 15 minutes, turning often and basting frequently with the remaining marinade.

TIME: Preparation takes 10 minutes plus 2 hours marinating. Cooking takes about 15 minutes.

COOK'S TIP: Allow the meat to come to room temperature before cooking.

Chicken and Sausage Risotto

This is really a one pot meal and one you won't have to cook in the oven.

SERVES 4-6

1.5kg/3lbs chicken portions, skinned, boned, and cut into cubes
45g/1½oz butter or margarine
1 large onion, roughly chopped
3 sticks celery, roughly chopped
1 large green pepper, roughly chopped
1 clove garlic, crushed
Salt and pepper
225g/8oz uncooked rice
400g/14oz canned tomatoes
180g/6oz smoked sausage, cut into 1.25cm/½-inch dice
850ml/1½ pints chicken stock
Chopped parsley

1. Use the chicken skin and bones and the onion and celery trimmings to make stock. Cover the ingredients with water, bring to the boil and then simmer slowly for 1 hour. Strain and reserve.

2. Melt the butter or margarine in a large saucepan and add the onion. Cook slowly to brown and then add the celery, green pepper and garlic and cook briefly.

3. Add the salt and pepper and the rice, stirring to mix well.

4. Add the chicken, tomatoes, sausage and stock and mix well. Bring to the boil, then reduce the heat to simmering and cook for about 20-25 minutes, stirring occasionally, until the chicken is done and the rice is tender. The rice should have absorbed most of the liquid by the time it has cooked. Sprinkle in the chopped parsley to serve.

TIME: Preparation takes about 1 hour and cooking takes about 30-35 minutes.

PREPARATION: Check the level of liquid occasionally as the rice is cooking and add more water or stock as necessary. If there is a lot of liquid left and the rice is nearly cooked, uncover the pan and boil rapidly.

SERVING IDEAS: Add a green salad to make a complete meal.

Plaice and Mushroom Turnovers

These delicious individual pies make a warming family lunch or supper dish.

SERVES 4

4 plaice fillets, skinned
Salt and pepper
120ml/4 fl oz milk
120g/4oz button mushrooms, trimmed and thinly sliced
30g/1oz butter
Juice of 1 lemon
3 tbsps hazelnut, or lemon, stuffing mix
350g/12oz puff pastry
Beaten egg, for glazing
Poppy seeds, for sprinkling

1. Season the plaice fillets and roll them up swiss roll fashion. Secure each roll with a wooden cocktail stick and poach gently in the milk for about 10 minutes in a preheated oven, 180°C/350°F/Gas Mark 4.

2. Drain the fish and allow it to cool. Remove the cocktail sticks. Increase the oven temperature to 200°C/400°F/ Gas Mark 6.

3. Put the mushrooms and butter into a pan with the lemon juice. Cook over a moderate heat for about 5 minutes.

4. Allow the mushrooms to cool and then stir in the stuffing mix.

5. Roll out the pastry, quite thinly, into 4 circles, each 15cm/6 inches in diameter. Brush the edges with beaten egg.

6. Put a fish roll into the centre of each pastry circle and top with a quarter of the mushroom mixture. Pull the pastry edges up and over the fish and pinch together to seal.

7. Place the turnovers on a greased baking sheet and glaze with the beaten egg. Sprinkle with a few poppy seeds.

8. Bake in the reset oven for about 25 minutes, or until well risen, puffed and golden. Serve piping hot.

TIME Preparation will take about 25 minutes, plus the cooling time. Cooking will take about 35 minutes.

Pastitsio

This is like an Italian version of Shepherd's Pie with tomatoes in the mince and macaroni instead of potato.

SERVES 4

225g/8oz package macaroni
90g/3oz butter or margarine
60g/2oz Parmesan cheese, grated
Pinch of grated nutmeg
2 eggs, beaten
1 medium onion, peeled and chopped
1 clove garlic, crushed
450g/1lb minced beef
2 tbsps tomato purée
60ml/2fl oz red wine
90ml/3fl oz beef stock
2 tbsps chopped parsley
2 tbsps plain flour
280ml/½ pint milk
Salt
Pepper

1. Preheat oven to 190°C/375°F/Gas Mark 5.

2. Cook macaroni in plenty of boiling salted water for 10 minutes, or until tender but still firm. Rinse under hot water. Drain.

3. Put one-third of the butter in the pan and return macaroni to it. Add half the cheese, nutmeg, and salt and pepper to taste. Leave to cool. Mix in half the beaten egg, and put aside.

4. Melt half of the remaining butter in a pan, and fry the onion and garlic gently until onion is soft. Increase temperature, add meat, and fry until browned.

5. Add tomato purée, stock, parsley and wine, and season with salt and pepper. Simmer for 20 minutes.

6. In a small pan, melt the rest of the butter. Stir in the flour and cook for 30 seconds. Remove from heat, and stir in milk. Bring to boil, stirring continuously, until the sauce thickens.

7. Beat in the remaining egg and season to taste. Spoon half the macaroni into a serving dish and cover with the meat sauce.

8. Put on another layer of macaroni and smooth over. Pour over white sauce, sprinkle with remaining cheese, and bake in the oven for 30 minutes until golden brown. Serve immediately.

TIME: Preparation takes 10 minutes and cooking takes 1 hour.

Fried Chicken

Fried Chicken is easy to make at home and it's much better than a take away!

SERVES 4

2 eggs
1.5kg/3lb chicken portions
225g/8oz flour
1 tsp each salt, paprika and sage
½ tsp black pepper
Pinch cayenne pepper (optional)
Oil for frying
Parsley or watercress to garnish

1. Beat the eggs in a large bowl and add the chicken one piece at a time, turning to coat.

2. Mix flour and seasonings in a large plastic bag.

3. Place the chicken into the bag one piece at a time, close bag tightly and shake to coat. Alternatively, dip each chicken piece in a bowl of seasoned flour, shaking off the excess.

4. Heat about 1.25cm/½ inch of oil in a large frying pan.

5. When the oil is hot, add the chicken skin side down first. Fry for about 12 minutes and then turn over. Fry a further 12 minutes or until the juices run clear.

6. Drain the chicken on kitchen paper and serve immediately. Garnish with parsley or watercress.

TIME: Preparation takes about 20 minutes and cooking takes about 24 minutes.

PREPARATION: The chicken should not be crowded in the frying pan. If the pan is small, fry the chicken in several batches.

COOK'S TIP: When coating anything for frying, be sure to coat it just before cooking. If left to stand, the coating will usually become very soggy.

Chilli con Carne

Although this dish is Mexican in origin, the version everyone knows best is really more American.

SERVES 4

1 tbsp oil
460g/1lb minced beef
2 tsps ground cumin
2 tsps mild or hot chilli powder
Pinch oregano
Salt, pepper and pinch sugar
¼ tsp garlic powder
2 tbsps flour
460g/1lb canned tomatoes
460g/1lb canned red kidney beans
Boiled rice, to serve

1. Heat the oil in a large saucepan and brown the meat, breaking it up with a fork as it cooks.

2. Sprinkle on the cumin, chilli powder, oregano, salt, pepper and sugar, garlic and flour. Cook, stirring frequently, over a medium heat for about 3 minutes.

3. Add the tomatoes and their liquid and simmer for 25-30 minutes.

4. Drain the kidney beans and add just before serving, heating through for about 5 minutes.

TIME: Preparation takes about 15 minutes. Cooking takes about 10 minutes to brown the meat and 25-30 minutes to cook after the tomatoes are added.

SERVING IDEAS: Spoon the chilli on top of boiled rice to serve. Top with a combination of soured cream, chopped onion, grated cheese and diced avocado. Accompany with tortillas.

TO FREEZE: Allow the chilli to cool completely and place in rigid containers, seal, label and freeze for up to 3 months. Thaw completely before reheating.

CHICKEN COBBLER

This dish is warming winter fare with its creamy sauce and tender, light topping.

SERVES 6

4 chicken joints: 2 breasts and 2 legs
1.5 litres/2½ pints water
1 bay leaf
4 whole peppercorns
2 carrots, peeled and diced
24 button onions, peeled
90g/6 tbsps frozen sweetcorn
140ml/¼ pint double cream
Salt

Cobbler Topping
400g/14oz plain flour
1½ tbsps baking powder
Pinch salt
75g/2½oz butter or margarine
340ml/12 fl oz milk
1 egg, beaten with a pinch of salt

1. Place the chicken in a deep saucepan with the water, bay leaf and peppercorns. Cover and bring to the boil. Reduce the heat and allow to simmer for 20-30 minutes, or until the chicken is tender. Remove the chicken from the pan and allow to cool. Skim and discard the fat from the surface of the stock.

2. Continue to simmer the stock until reduced by about half. Meanwhile, skin the chicken and remove the meat from the bones. Strain the stock and add the carrots and onions. Cook until tender and add the sweetcorn. Stir in the cream, season and add the chicken. Pour into a warmed casserole or into individual baking dishes and keep hot.

3. To prepare the topping, sift the dry ingredients into a bowl or place them in a food processor and process once or twice to sift.

4. Rub in the butter or margarine until the mixture resembles breadcrumbs. Stir in enough of the milk until the mixture comes together. If using a food processor trickle the milk in down the food tube and process in short bursts to avoid overmixing.

5. Turn out onto a floured surface and knead lightly. Roll out with a floured rolling pin until it is about 1.25cm/½-inch thick.

6. Cut the dough into rounds using a 5cm/2-inch cutter to form the cobbles. Place the rounds on top of the chicken mixture and brush the surface of the cobbler with the egg and salt mixture and bake for 10-15 minutes in a pre-heated oven at 190°C/375°F/Gas Mark 5. Serve immediately.

TIME: Preparation takes about 20-30 minutes for the chicken, about 20 minutes to prepare the sauce, and the cobbler takes about 10 minutes to prepare. Final cooking takes about 10-15 minutes.

PREPARATION: Once the topping has been prepared it must be baked immediately or the baking powder will stop working and the cobbler topping will not rise.

Sweet and Sour Pork and Pineapple

A classic Chinese recipe that is easy to prepare at home.

SERVES 4

450g/1lb lean pork fillet, cut into 2.5cm/1-inch cubes
2 tbsps light soy sauce
2 tbsps white wine vinegar
2 tbsps tomato purée
1 tbsp sugar
2 tbsps peanut oil
1 tbsp cornflour
1 clove garlic, crushed
1 tsp grated root ginger
140ml/¼ pint water
1 can pineapple pieces, drained
Fresh coriander to garnish

1. Place the pork in bowl, pour over light soy sauce and toss together. Leave to marinate for 15 minutes.

2. Meanwhile, make the sauce, by mixing together the vinegar, tomato purée and sugar, and set aside.

3. Heat a wok and add the oil.

4. Remove pork from soy sauce, and add soy sauce to sauce mixture. Toss pork in cornflour, coating well.

5. When oil is hot, brown pork well all over. Remove from pan and reduce heat.

6. Fry garlic and ginger for 30 seconds. Add water. Bring to the boil, then return pork to wok.

7. Reduce heat; cover and simmer for 15 minutes, stirring occasionally.

8. Add sauce mixture and pineapple, and simmer for a further 15 minutes. Garnish with coriander.

TIME: Preparation takes 15 minutes and cooking takes about 20 minutes.

WATCHPOINT: Take care when you add the water to the wok.

SERVING IDEAS: Serve with rice and prawn crackers.

Cheese and Tomato Pasta

This favourite Italian classic is perfect served as a supper dish and will be popular with all the family.

SERVES 4

225g/8oz tagliatelle verdi
Salt
1 tbsp vegetable oil
1 onion, chopped
120g/4oz mushrooms, finely sliced
1 tbsp tomato purée
1 × 400g/14oz can chopped tomatoes
2 tbsps dried mixed herbs
120g/4oz vegetarian Cheddar cheese, grated
Freshly ground black pepper

1. Cook the pasta in plenty of lightly salted boiling water for 10 minutes, until 'al dente' or as directed on the packet.

2. Meanwhile, heat the oil and sauté the onions until beginning to soften.

3. Add the mushrooms and sauté for 3 minutes. Stir in the tomato purée, tomatoes and herbs, and simmer gently whilst the pasta cooks.

4. When the pasta is cooked, stir most of the cheese into the tomato sauce. Season.

5. Drain the pasta well and pile onto a serving dish. Spoon the sauce into the centre and top with the remaining cheese.

TIME: Preparation takes about 10 minutes, cooking takes about 20 minutes.

COOK'S TIP: Fresh pasta is now readily available and very quick to cook. You will need about twice the weight of dried pasta.

SERVING IDEA: Serve with a mixed salad and hot garlic bread.

VARIATION: Use any variety of pasta shapes in this recipe.

Lamb Korma

One of the best known Indian curries, a korma is rich, spicy and a traditional favourite.

SERVES 4

3 tbsps vegetable oil
1 medium onion, sliced
2.5cm/1 inch piece cinnamon stick
6 cloves
Seeds of 6 small cardamoms
1 bay leaf
1 tsp black cumin seeds
2 tsps ginger paste, or grated fresh ginger
1 tsp garlic paste, or 2 cloves garlic, crushed
450g/1lb shoulder of lamb, cubed
1 tsp chilli powder
1 tsp ground coriander
2 tsps ground cumin
½ tsp ground turmeric
140ml/¼ pint natural yogurt
160ml/6fl oz water
Salt to taste
1 tbsp ground almonds
2 green chillies, halved and seeded
2 sprigs fresh coriander leaves, chopped

1. Fry the onion in the oil until golden brown. Add the cinnamon, cloves, cardamoms, bay leaf and the cumin seeds. Fry for 1 minute.

2. Add the ginger and garlic pastes and the cubed lamb. Sprinkle over the chilli powder, ground coriander, cumin and turmeric and mix together well.

3. Stir in the yogurt, cover the pan and cook over a moderate heat for 10-15 minutes, stirring occasionally.

4. Add the water and salt to taste, re-cover and simmer gently for 30-40 minutes, or until the meat is tender.

5. Just before serving, add the almonds, chillies and coriander leaves. Stir in a little more water if necessary, to produce a medium-thick gravy.

TIME: Preparation takes about 15 minutes, and cooking takes about 40-50 minutes.

SERVING IDEA: Serve with boiled rice, or chapattis.

Piquant Pork Chops

The spicy sauce in this recipe completely transforms the humble pork chop.

SERVES 4

4 lean pork chops, trimmed of fat and rind
1 tbsp polyunsaturated vegetable oil
1 small onion, chopped
1 tbsp unrefined brown sugar
1 tbsp dry mustard, any flavour
2 tsps tomato purée
1 beef stock cube
280ml/½ pint water
1 tbsp Worcestershire sauce
2 tbsps fresh lemon juice

1. Grill the pork chops under a preheated hot grill for 6-7 minutes on each side.

2. Heat the oil in a large frying pan, and fry the onion gently, until it is lightly browned.

3. Stir the sugar, mustard powder, tomato purée and beef stock cube into the cooked onion. Mix the ingredients together well, then add the water and bring to the boil, stirring continuously.

4. Stir the Worcestershire sauce and the lemon juice into the onion and spice mixture, then check the seasoning, adding freshly ground sea salt and black pepper to taste.

5. Put the pork chops into an ovenproof baking dish, or shallow casserole, and pour the sauce over them.

6. Cook in a preheated oven, 180°C/350°F/Gas Mark 4, for about 40-45 minutes, or until the meat is tender.

Time: Preparation takes about 30 minutes, and cooking takes about 1 hour.

Serving Idea: Serve with creamed potatoes and green vegetables.

Chicken Cacciatore

The use of herbs, wine and vinegar in this delicious Italian family meal gives a wonderful, hearty flavour. Serve with rice or pasta and a mixed salad.

SERVES 4-6

60ml/4 tbsps olive oil
1.4kg/3lbs chicken pieces
2 onions, sliced
3 cloves garlic, crushed
225g/8oz button mushrooms, quartered
140ml/¼ pint red wine
1 tbsp wine vinegar
1 tbsp fresh chopped parsley
2 tsps fresh chopped oregano
2 tsps fresh chopped basil
1 bay leaf
450g/1lb canned tomatoes
140ml/¼ pint chicken stock
Salt and freshly ground black pepper
Pinch of sugar

1. In a large frying pan heat the oil and add the chicken pieces, skin side down, in one layer.

2. Brown for 3-4 minutes, then turn each piece over. Continue turning the chicken portions until all surfaces are well browned.

3. Remove the chicken portions to a plate and keep warm.

4. Add the onions and garlic to the oil and chicken juices in the frying pan. Cook lightly for 2-3 minutes, or until they are just beginning to brown.

5. Add the mushrooms to the pan and cook for about 1 minute, stirring constantly.

6. Pour the wine and vinegar into the pan and boil rapidly to reduce to about half the original quantity.

7. Add the herbs, bay leaf and tomatoes, stirring well to break up the tomatoes.

8. Stir in the chicken stock and season with salt and pepper and sugar.

9. Return the chicken to the tomato sauce and cover with a tight-fitting lid. Simmer for about 1 hour, or until the chicken is tender.

TIME: Preparation takes about 30 minutes, cooking takes 1 hour.

VARIATIONS: Use the delicious sauce in this recipe with any other meat of your choice.

TO FREEZE: This dish freezes well for up to 3 months. Defrost thoroughly and reheat by bringing to the boil then simmering for at least 30 minutes before serving.

Oven Baked Spaghetti

A convenient way to cook this favourite mid-week meal.

SERVES 4

225g/8oz wholewheat spaghetti, cooked
2 × 400g/14oz tins tomatoes, roughly chopped
1 large onion, grated
1 tsp oregano
Seasoning
120g/4oz Cheddar cheese
2 tbsps grated Parmesan cheese

1. Grease four individual ovenproof dishes and place a quarter of the spaghetti in each one.

2. Pour the tomatoes over the top.

3. Add the onion, sprinkle with oregano and season well.

4. Slice the cheese finely and arrange over the top of the spaghetti mixture.

5. Sprinkle with Parmesan and bake at 180°C/350°F/Gas Mark 4 for 20-25 minutes.

TIME: Preparation takes 10 minutes, cooking takes 20-25 minutes.

SERVING IDEAS: Serve with garlic bread.

WATCHPOINT: When cooking spaghetti remember to add a few drops of oil to the boiling water to stop it sticking together.

COOK'S TIP: Oven Baked Spaghetti may be cooked in one large casserole if required, but add 10 minutes to the cooking time.

Chicken, Ham and Leek Pie

The addition of cream and egg yolks at the end of the cooking time makes this pie extra special.

SERVES 6-8

1 × 1.5kg/3lb chicken
1 onion
1 bay leaf
Parsley stalks
Salt and black pepper
450g/1lb leeks
30g/1oz butter
120g/4oz cooked ham, chopped
1 tbsp parsley
280ml/½ pint chicken stock
340-400g/12-14oz puff pastry
140ml/¼ pint double cream
1 egg, lightly beaten for glazing

1. Put the cleaned chicken in a large saucepan together with the onion, bay leaf, parsley stalks and salt and pepper. Cover with cold water and bring gently to the boil. Allow to simmer for about 45 minutes until the chicken is tender. Leave it to cool in the pan.

2. Meanwhile, wash and trim the leeks and cut into 3.75cm/1½-inch pieces. Melt the butter in a small pan and gently sauté the leeks for about 5 minutes. Remove from the heat.

3. Take the cooled chicken out of the pan, remove the skin and strip off the flesh. Cut it into good-sized pieces.

4. Put the chicken, ham, leeks and parsley into a large pie dish with plenty of seasoning. Pour over 280ml/½ pint of the stock from the chicken.

5. Roll out the pastry slightly larger than the size of the pie dish. Use the trimmings to line the rim of the dish. Dampen them and put on the pastry lid. Trim and seal the edges together firmly. Any surplus pastry can be used to make decorative leaves. Cut a few slits in the pastry to allow the steam to escape. Brush the pastry well with beaten egg.

6. Bake in the centre of a preheated 230°C/450°F/Gas Mark 8 oven for 15 minutes, remove and glaze again with beaten egg. Reduce the temperature of the oven to 200°C/400°F/Gas Mark 6. Return the pie to the oven for another 20 minutes.

7. When the pie crust is well risen and golden brown, remove it from the oven and carefully lift off a segment of pastry and pour in the cream which has been gently warmed together with the remaining beaten egg.

TIME: Preparation takes about 45 minutes for the chicken plus extra cooling time and 20 minutes to prepare the pie. Cooking takes about 35 minutes.

SERVING IDEAS: Serve with creamed potatoes and a green vegetable.

COLCANNON

This traditional Irish dish of potatoes, cabbage and onion is a wonderful combination and makes a change from ordinary mashed potatoes.

SERVES 4

90g/3oz finely chopped onion, leek or spring onions
30g/1oz polyunsaturated margarine
60ml/2 fl oz skimmed milk
460g/1lb cooked potatoes, mashed
225g/8oz cooked cabbage

1. Melt the margarine in a pan, add the onion, leek or spring onions and gently sauté until soft.

2. Add the milk and the well-mashed potatoes and stir until heated through.

3. Chop the cabbage finely and beat into the mixture over a low heat until all the mixture is pale green and fluffy.

TIME: Preparation takes 30 minutes, including cooking the vegetables. Cooking takes 10 minutes.

Stir-Fried Vegetable Medley

Stir-frying is a very good method of cooking vegetables as it is so brief. When cooked the vegetables should still be slightly crunchy.

SERVES 4

2 carrots
225g/8oz broccoli
1 onion
1 courgette
2 celery sticks
2 tbsps oil
¼ tsp finely grated fresh root ginger
1 clove garlic, crushed
1 can baby sweetcorn, drained
1 tbsp light soy sauce
Salt and pepper

1. Cut the carrots into flowers by cutting out 5 small V-shaped grooves lengthwise around the carrots. Cut carrots crosswise into rounds.

2. Divide broccoli into small florets and slit the stems to ensure quick cooking.

3. Slice onion into julienne strips.

4. Diagonally slice the courgette and celery.

5. Heat a wok and add the oil. Add ginger, garlic, onion, carrots, broccoli and courgette, and toss in oil for 2-3 minutes.

6. Add the celery and baby sweetcorn, and toss 1-2 minutes longer.

7. Season with soy sauce, and salt and pepper if wished.

TIME: Preparation takes about 20 minutes and cooking takes 4-5 minutes.

PREPARATION: Make sure that you prepare all the ingredients before starting to cook this dish.

COOK'S TIP: Add some cornflour, blended with a little water, to thicken the vegetable juices if necessary.

Bavarian Potato Salad

It is best to prepare this salad a few hours in advance to allow the potatoes to absorb the flavours.

SERVES 4-6

900g/2lbs tiny new potatoes
4 tbsps olive oil
4 spring onions, finely chopped
1 clove garlic, crushed
2 tbsps fresh dill, chopped or 1 tbsp dried
2 tbsps wine vinegar
½ tsp sugar
Seasoning
2 tbsps chopped fresh parsley

1. Wash the potatoes but do not peel, put them into a pan, cover with water and boil until just tender.

2. Whilst the potatoes are cooking, heat the olive oil in a frying pan and cook the spring onions and garlic for 2-3 minutes until they have softened a little.

3. Add the dill and cook gently for a further minute.

4. Add the wine vinegar and sugar, and stir until the sugar melts. Remove from the heat and add a little seasoning.

5. Drain the potatoes and pour the dressing over them whilst they are still hot.

6. Allow to cool and sprinkle with the chopped parsley before serving.

TIME: Preparation takes 15 minutes, cooking takes 15 minutes.

SERVING IDEA: Serve with cold roasts.

2lb

Prawn Egg Rice

Serve this on its own for a tasty lunch or supper dish, or as part of a more elaborate Chinese meal.

SERVES 6

450g/1lb long grain rice
2 eggs
½ tsp salt
60ml/4 tbsps oil
1 large onion, chopped
2 cloves of garlic, chopped
120g/4oz peeled prawns
60g/2oz frozen peas
2 spring onions, chopped
2 tbsps dark soy sauce

1. Wash the rice thoroughly and put it in a wok. Add water to come 2.5cm/1 inch above the top of the rice.

2. Bring the rice to the boil, stir once, then reduce the heat. Cover and simmer the rice for 5-7 minutes, or until the liquid has been absorbed.

3. Rinse the rice in cold water and fluff up with a fork, to separate the grains.

4. Beat the eggs with a pinch of salt. Heat 1 tbsp of the oil in the wok and cook the onion until soft, but not brown. Pour in the egg and stir gently, until the mixture is set. Remove the egg mixture and set it aside.

5. Heat a further tablespoon of the oil and fry the garlic, prawns, peas and spring onions quickly for 2 minutes. Remove from the wok and set aside.

6. Heat the remaining oil in the wok and stir in the rice and remaining salt. Stir-fry, to heat the rice through, then add the egg and the prawn mixtures and the soy sauce, stirring to blend thoroughly. Serve immediately.

TIME: Preparation takes about 20 minutes and cooking takes about 15 minutes.

VARIATIONS: Use chopped red peppers or corn kernels, instead of the peas.

Creamy Sweetcorn and Peppers

Sweetcorn is essential to this recipe, but other vegetables can be added, too. Choose your favourites or use what you have to hand.

SERVES 6

60ml/4 tbsps oil
30g/1oz butter
2 medium onions, finely chopped
1 clove garlic, crushed
1 medium green pepper, cut into small dice
6 tomatoes, skinned, seeded and diced
225g/8oz frozen corn kernels
280ml/½ pint chicken or vegetable stock
Pinch salt
60ml/4 tbsps double cream
Pinch of paprika

1. Heat the oil in a large casserole and add the butter. When foaming, add the onions and garlic and cook, stirring frequently, for about 5 minutes or until both are soft and transparent but not browned.

2. Add the green pepper, tomatoes, corn and stock. Bring to the boil over high heat.

3. Reduce the heat, partially cover the casserole and allow to cook slowly for about 10 minutes, or until the corn is tender. Add salt and stir in the cream. Heat through, sprinkle with paprika and serve immediately.

TIME: Preparation takes about 25 minutes. Cooking takes about 10 minutes.

VARIATIONS: Use canned tomatoes, coarsely chopped.

COOK'S TIP: Sweetcorn toughens if cooked at too high a temperature for too long, or if boiled too rapidly.

Potatoes with Poppy Seeds

This quick and easy, but thoroughly delicious, potato dish comes from Assam. Serve it as a side dish or as a snack – simply gorgeous!

SERVES 4-6

5 tbsps cooking oil
½ tsp Kalonji (onion seeds), optional
1 tsp cumin seeds
4-6 cloves garlic, peeled and crushed
1 tsp freshly ground black pepper
½ tsp ground turmeric
700g/1½lbs potatoes, peeled and diced
1 fresh green chilli, finely chopped
6 tbsps white poppy seeds
1 tsp salt or to taste

1. Heat the oil in a non-stick or cast iron pan until smoking. Remove the pan from heat and add the kalonji (if used) and cumin seeds.

2. As soon as the seeds start crackling, add the garlic and place the pan over medium heat.

3. Add the ground black pepper and turmeric, stir briskly and add the potatoes and the green chilli. Fry the potatoes for 2-3 minutes stirring constantly.

4. Reduce heat to low, cover the pan and cook until the potatoes are tender (12-15 minutes), stirring occasionally.

5. Meanwhile, grind the poppy seeds in a coffee grinder into a coarse mixture. Add this to the potatoes, adjust heat to medium and fry the potato and poppy seed mixture for 5-6 minutes, stirring frequently.

6. Stir in the salt and remove the pan from heat.

TIME Preparation takes 10 minutes, cooking takes 20 minutes.

WATCHPOINT Make sure the potatoes are cut into small cubes, if cut into chunky pieces it will be difficult to cook them thoroughly in the specified time.
Use a non-stick or cast iron pan, otherwise the potatoes will stick.

De-Luxe Bread and Butter Pudding

Serve just as it is, hot from the oven.

SERVES 4

4 thin slices wholemeal bread
A little butter
Raspberry jam
2 eggs, beaten
420ml/¾ pint milk, warmed
2 tbsps single cream
3 tbsps light muscovado sugar
1 tsp vanilla essence
2 tbsps sultanas, soaked in water for 1 hour, drained
1 tbsp dates, chopped
Grated nutmeg

1. Remove the crusts from the bread.

2. Sandwich the bread with the butter and jam and cut into small triangles.

3. Beat the eggs until foamy.

4. Add the warmed milk, cream, sugar and vanilla

5. Stir together well, making sure that the sugar has dissolved.

6. Arrange the bread triangles in a lightly buttered ovenproof dish so that they overlap and stand up slightly.

7. Scatter the dried fruits over the top.

8. Pour the egg, cream and milk mixture into the dish, ensuring that the bread triangles are saturated.

9. Grate a little nutmeg over the pudding and bake in an oven preheated to 200°C/400°F/Gas Mark 6 for about 30 minutes.

TIME: Preparation takes 10 minutes, cooking takes 30 minutes.

VARIATION: Other flavoured jams may be used instead of raspberry jam.

BAKED APPLES IN OVERCOATS

Pastry sweetened with cinnamon and spices combines with a rich fruit filling to make this warming winter dessert.

SERVES 6

340g/12oz plain flour
¼ tsp salt
¼ tsp cinnamon
¼ tsp ground nutmeg
175g/6oz butter
75-105ml/5-7 tbsps iced water
6 medium dessert apples
6 prunes, pitted
6 dried apricots
2 tbsps raisins
1 egg, beaten to glaze
Fresh mint, to decorate
Fresh cream, to serve

1. Sift the flour, salt and spices into a large bowl. Cut the butter into dice and rub into the flour until the mixture resembles fine breadcrumbs.

2. Mix in enough water to produce a smooth pliable dough. Divide the dough into six pieces and roll each out into a 20cm/8-inch square.

3. Peel the apples with a sharp knife and carefully remove the centre cores with an apple corer. Chop the prunes and the apricots and mix these with the raisins.

4. Place one prepared apple in the centre of each pastry square, and fill the cavities with equal amounts of the dried fruit mixture.

5. Brush the edges of each square with a little water, and draw them up and around the sides of the apples, sealing them well with a little water and trimming off any excess pastry to give a neat finish.

6. Roll out the pastry trimmings, cut into decorative leaves and stick the leaves onto each apple for decoration.

7. Glaze each pastry apple with the beaten egg and place on a lightly greased baking sheet.

8. Bake the apples in an oven preheated to 180°C/350°F/Gas Mark 4, for 20-25 minutes or until golden brown.

9. Decorate with sprigs of mint and serve hot with fresh cream or custard.

TIME: Preparation takes about 30 minutes, cooking time takes 20-25 minutes.

COOK'S TIP: For an extra rich pastry, use 1 egg yolk and half the amount of water in this recipe.

VARIATION: Use pears instead of apples in this recipe.

TO FREEZE: These apples freeze well after baking and should be thawed, then re-heated, before eating.

Zuppa Inglese

This is Italy's tribute to trifle. The name means English soup, but the custard is rich and thick.

SERVES 6-8

2 tbsps cornflour
570ml/1 pint milk
2 eggs, lightly beaten
2 tbsps sugar
Grated rind of ½ lemon
Pinch nutmeg
460g/1lb ripe strawberries
16 sponge fingers
Amaretto liqueur
140ml/¼ pint double cream

1. Mix the cornflour with some of the milk. Beat the eggs, sugar, lemon rind and nutmeg together and pour in the remaining milk. Mix with the cornflour mixture in a heavy-based pan and stir over gentle heat until the mixture thickens and comes to the boil.

2. Allow to boil for 1 minute or until the mixture coats the back of a spoon. Place a sheet of greaseproof paper directly on top of the custard and allow it to cool slightly.

3. Save 8 even-sized strawberries for decoration and hull the remaining ones. Place half of the sponge fingers in the bottom of a large glass bowl and sprinkle with some amaretto.

4. Cut the strawberries in half and place a layer on top of the sponge fingers. Pour a layer of custard on top and repeat with the remaining sliced strawberries and sponge fingers. Top with another layer of custard and allow to cool completely.

5. Whip the cream and spread a thin layer over the top of the set custard. Pipe the remaining cream around the edge of the dish and decorate with the reserved strawberries. Serve chilled.

TIME: Preparation takes about 20 minutes, custard takes about 5 minutes to cook.

VARIATIONS: Decorate the top of the dessert with grated chocolate, toasted almonds or shelled pistachios in addition to, or instead of, the strawberries. Other fruit may be used, if wished.

LAZZARONI

Lemon and Ginger Cheesecake

This fresh, creamy-tasting cheesecake is full of wholesome ingredients.

SERVES 6-8

45g/1½oz butter or margarine, melted
30g/1oz soft brown sugar
90g/3oz wholemeal biscuits, crushed
175g/6oz low fat soft cheese
2 eggs, separated
Finely grated rind 1 lemon
30g/1oz soft brown sugar
140ml/¼ pint natural yogurt, or fromage frais
15g/½oz powdered gelatine
3 tbsps hot water
Juice ½ lemon
3 pieces preserved stem ginger, rinsed in warm water and chopped
60ml/4 tbsps thick natural yogurt, or fromage frais
Fine matchstick strips lemon peel, or twists of lemon, to decorate

1. Lightly grease an 18cm/7-inch flan dish.

2. Mix the melted butter with the soft brown sugar and the crushed biscuits. Press the biscuit crumb mixture evenly over the base of the dish.

3. Chill the biscuit base, for at least 1 hour, in the refrigerator.

4. Beat the soft cheese with the egg yolks, lemon rind and sugar. Stir in the yogurt.

5. Dissolve the gelatine in the water, and add this in a thin stream to the cheese mixture, stirring thoroughly, to incorporate evenly.

6. Stir in the lemon juice and put the cheese mixture to one side until it is on the point of setting.

7. Whisk the egg whites until they are stiff but not dry and fold these lightly, but thoroughly, into the cheese mixture together with the chopped stem ginger.

8. Spoon this mixture into the prepared flan dish, smoothing the surface level.

9. Chill the cheesecake for 3-4 hours until the filling has set completely. Swirl the natural yogurt over the top of the cheesecake and decorate with the strips of lemon peel, or lemon twists.

TIME: Preparation takes about 30 minutes, plus 1 hour chilling time. The finished dish requires 3-4 hours refrigeration before serving.

COOK'S TIP: The gelatine will dissolve more quickly if you sprinkle it onto the hot water in a small bowl, and stand this bowl in a larger bowl of hot water. Stir the gelatine to ensure that no grainy bits remain.

Brown Sugar Bananas

Bananas in a rich brown sugar sauce make a delectable dessert.

SERVES 4

4 ripe bananas, peeled
Lemon juice
120g/4oz butter
120g/4oz soft brown sugar, light or dark
Pinch ground cinnamon and nutmeg
140ml/¼ pint orange juice
60ml/4 tbsps white or dark rum
Juice of ½ lemon
140ml/¼ pint whipped cream
2 tbsps chopped pecans

1. Cut the bananas in half lengthwise and sprinkle with lemon juice on all sides.

2. Melt the butter in a large frying pan and add the sugar, cinnamon, nutmeg and orange juice. Stir over gentle heat until the sugar dissolves into a syrup.

3. Add the banana halves and cook gently for about 3 minutes, basting the bananas often with syrup, but not turning them.

4. Once the bananas are heated through, warm the rum in a small saucepan and ignite with a match. Pour the flaming rum over the bananas and shake the pan gently until the flames die down naturally. Place 2 banana halves on each serving plate and top with some of the whipped cream. Sprinkle with pecans and serve immediately.

TIME: Preparation takes about 15 minutes and cooking takes about 5 minutes for the sugar and butter syrup and 3-4 minutes for the bananas.

SERVING IDEAS: The bananas may be served with vanilla ice cream instead of whipped cream, if wished.

COOK'S TIP: Sprinkling the cut surfaces of the banana with lemon juice keeps them from turning brown and also offsets the sweetness of the sauce.

Chocolate Cream Helène

Pears, cream and pasta combine perfectly in this simply delicious dessert.

SERVES 4

90g/3oz soup pasta
450ml/¾ pint milk
45g/1½ oz caster sugar
1 tsp cocoa
140ml/¼ pint cream, lightly whipped
1 tbsp hot water
1 large tin pear halves

Garnish
Chocolate, grated

1. Cook pasta in milk and sugar until soft. Stir regularly, being careful not to allow it to boil over.

2. Meanwhile, dissolve cocoa in hot water, and stir into pasta.

3. Pour pasta into a bowl to cool, when cool, fold in lightly-whipped cream. Chill. Serve with pear halves, and a sprinkling of grated chocolate.

TIME: Preparation takes 15 minutes and cooking takes 10 minutes.

Apple Nut Tart

The sweet, spicy flavour of cinnamon blends perfectly with the apples and nuts in this traditional dessert.

SERVES 6

250g/9oz plain flour
150g/5oz caster sugar
135g/4½ oz butter, cut into pieces
1 egg
450g/1lb dessert apples, peeled, cored and sliced
60g/2oz hazelnuts, coarsely ground
1 tsp ground cinnamon
Juice of 1 lemon
3 tbsps apricot brandy (optional)
120g/4oz apricot jam
60g/2oz chopped hazelnuts

1. Sieve together the flour and 120g/4oz of the sugar into a bowl. Rub in the butter until the mixture resembles fine breadcrumbs.

2. Make a well in the centre of the flour mixture, add the egg and mix using a knife or, as the mixture becomes firmer, your fingers. Continue kneading the until it forms a smooth dough.

3. Wrap the dough in greaseproof paper and chill for at least 30 minutes in the refrigerator.

4. Roll out the pastry and use it to line a 20cm/8 inch greased pie dish.

5. Layer the apple slices and the ground hazelnuts in the pastry case. Sprinkle over the cinnamon, remaining sugar, lemon juice and apricot brandy if using.

6. Put the apricot jam into a small saucepan and heat through gently until it has melted. Pour the melted jam over the layers of apple and hazelnut.

7. Sprinkle with the chopped hazelnuts and bake in a preheated oven, 220°C/425°F/Gas Mark 7, for 35-40 minutes, or until the fruit is soft and the tart is golden brown.

TIME: Preparation takes about 20 minutes, and cooking takes about 40 minutes.

SERVING IDEA: Serve with clotted cream.

Mexican Chocolate Flan

Flan in Mexico is a moulded custard with a caramel sauce. Chocolate and cinnamon is a favourite flavour combination.

SERVES 4

120g/4oz caster sugar
2 tbsps water
Juice of ½ lime
60g/2oz plain chocolate
280ml/½ pint milk
1 cinnamon stick
2 whole eggs
2 egg yolks
60g/4 tbsps sugar

1. Combine the first amount of sugar with the water and lime juice in a small, heavy-based saucepan.

2. Cook over a gentle heat, stirring until the sugar dissolves, then without stirring, bring the syrup to the boil and cook until golden brown and caramelized.

3. While preparing the syrup, heat 4 ramekins in an oven preheated to 180°C/350°F/Gas Mark 4. When the syrup is ready, pour into the hot ramekins and swirl to coat the sides and base evenly. Leave to cool at room temperature.

4. Chop the chocolate into small pieces and heat with the milk and cinnamon, stirring occasionally to help the chocolate dissolve.

5. Whisk the whole eggs and the yolks together with the remaining sugar until slightly frothy. Gradually whisk in the hot chocolate milk. Remove the cinnamon stick.

6. Strain the chocolate custard carefully into the ramekins and stand them in a roasting tin filled with enough hand-hot water to come half way up the sides of the dishes.

7. Carefully place the roasting tin in the oven, and bake the custards for 20-25 minutes, or until they have just set, and a knife inserted in the centre of the custard comes out clean.

8. Cool at room temperature and refrigerate for several hours or overnight before serving. Loosen the custards by running a knife around the edges and invert onto individual serving plates. If necessary shake the custard to allow it to drop out.

TIME: Preparation takes about 30 minutes, cooking takes about 35-40 minutes. Plus overnight chilling.

VARIATION: Leave out the chocolate, if wished, for a cinnamon flan.

WATCHPOINT: Do not allow the custard to overcook or it will form a tough skin on top. If the oven temperature is too high, it will cause the custard to boil and spoil the smooth texture.

SERVING IDEAS: Garnish with pecans or chocolate curls. Also good with fruit such as raspberries or bananas (with chocolate flan); peaches or strawberries (with cinnamon flan).

Fruit Kebabs

These unusual kebabs make the ideal dessert for a barbecue.

SERVES 4

4 peaches or apricots, halved
Small punnet strawberries
3-4 kiwi fruit, sliced
3-4 slices fresh pineapple, segmented
Mint leaves (optional)
Lemon juice
Honey

1. Thread alternate pieces of fruit onto skewers, interspersed with some fresh mint leaves.

2. Sprinkle with a little lemon juice and brush with some honey.

3. Barbecue for about 8 minutes.

TIME: Preparation takes about 15 minutes and cooking takes 8 minutes.

VARIATION: Use other fruit such as apples, mango, figs, bananas, paw paw, or nectarines.

SERVING IDEA: Serve with whipped cream or greek yogurt.

SUMMER PUDDING

This dessert must be prepared at least 24 hours before it is needed and is an excellent way of using up a glut of soft summer fruits. Most soft fruits can be used, but raspberries and redcurrants should predominate, both for taste and final colour.

SERVES 6

900g/2lbs mixed soft fruit (i.e. raspberries, redcurrants, blackcurrants, strawberries)
8 slices day-old white bread with crusts removed
120g/4oz caster sugar (more or less can be used according to taste)

1. Prepare and wash the fruit and place in a heavy-based saucepan together with the caster sugar. Cook over a low heat for 5-10 minutes until the sugar dissolves and the juices start to run.

2. Line the base and sides of a greased 1 litre/1¾ pint pudding basin with some of the slices of bread, trimming the slices so they fit tightly.

3. Pack in the fruit and enough juice to stain the bread. Cover with the remaining slices, pour on a little more juice and retain the rest.

4. Cover the basin with a saucer or plate which rests on the pudding itself. Add a 460g/1lb weight or heavy tin or jar, in order to compress the pudding. Leave to stand overnight in the refrigerator.

5. To turn out, loosen the sides with a palette knife and invert onto a serving plate.

TIME: Preparation takes about 20 minutes plus about 10 minutes cooking time. The pudding must be refrigerated for at least 24 hours before being served.

COOK'S TIP: Use the reserved juices to baste the unmoulded pudding to cover any white patches.

SERVING IDEA: Serve with double or clotted cream, and any remaining juice.

CHOCOLATE BROWNIES

These delectable chocolate bars with a fragile crusty top are a must for all chocaholics.

MAKES 9

90g/3oz plain flour
¼ tsp baking powder
Pinch salt
120g/4oz plain chocolate
60g/2oz butter
2 eggs
225g/8oz sugar
90g/3oz walnuts, chopped

1. Sift the flour, baking powder and salt together in a bowl.

2. Melt the chocolate and butter in a bowl over a small saucepan of hot water.

3. Beat the eggs with the sugar for 2 minutes until light and creamy.

4. Beat in the melted butter and chocolate, then fold in the flour and walnuts.

5. Grease and line a shallow 20cm/8-inch square tin and bake in an oven preheated to 160°C/325°F/Gas Mark 3, for 35 minutes. Cool in the tin and cut into squares.

TIME: Preparation takes about 25 minutes and cooking takes 35 minutes.

SERVING IDEA: Top with whipped cream or ice cream.

COOK'S TIP: Store in an air-tight container.

VARIATION: Use toasted chopped nuts.

ALMOND LAYER CAKE

Definitely not for the diet conscious, but delicious for those wishing to sin. This wonderful creamy gateau is ideal for serving with tea, or even as a dessert.

SERVES 8

60g/2oz dried white breadcrumbs
120ml/4 fl oz milk
2 tbsps rum
90g/3oz unsalted butter
90g/3oz caster sugar
6 eggs, separated
90g/3oz roasted almonds, ground
570ml/1 pint double cream
2 tbsps icing sugar
60g/2oz roasted almonds, finely chopped
Whole blanched almonds, lightly toasted, for decoration

1. Put the breadcrumbs into a large bowl and pour over the milk and half the rum. Allow to stand for 15 minutes or until the liquid has been completely absorbed.

2. Put the butter in a large bowl and beat until soft. Gradually add the sugar and continue mixing until it is light and fluffy.

3. Beat in the egg yolks, one at a time, mixing well to prevent it curdling. Fold in the soaked breadcrumbs to blend evenly.

4. Whisk the egg whites until they are stiff, but not dry. Fold these into the egg and butter mixture, along with the ground almonds.

5. Line and lightly grease 3 × 20cm/8-inch round cake tins, and dust each one lightly with a little flour.

6. Divide the cake mixture equally between the three tins. Bake in an oven preheated to 180°C/350°F/Gas Mark 4, for 30-35 minutes, or until well risen and golden brown.

7. Allow the cakes to cool briefly in the tins before gently loosening the sides and turning onto a wire rack to cool completely.

8. Whip the cream until it is stiff, then beat in the icing sugar and remaining rum.

9. Reserve one third of the cream and fold the finely chopped almonds into the rest.

10. Sandwich the cake layers together with the almond cream, then spread a thin layer of the plain cream onto the top, using the rest for piping rosettes of cream onto the top of the cake. Decorate with the toasted whole almonds and serve.

TIME: Preparation takes 40 minutes, cooking takes 35 minutes.

COOK'S TIP: Refrigerate the cream for at least 2 hours before whipppping, to obtain better results.

TO FREEZE: The almond cakes can be frozen for up to 1 month, but should be filled and decorated just before serving or they will become too soggy.

PEANUT BUTTER BRAN COOKIES

These rich, crumbly cookies are just the thing for hungry children.

MAKES ABOUT 35

120g/4oz butter or margarine
120g/4oz light muscovado sugar
1 egg, beaten
225g/8oz crunchy peanut butter
60g/2oz bran
120g/4oz wholemeal flour
Pinch salt
½ tsp baking powder
½ tsp vanilla essence

1. Beat together the butter and sugar until pale and creamy. Gradually add the egg, beating well after each addition.

2. Beat in the peanut butter, bran, flour, salt, baking powder and essence, mixing well to form a stiff dough.

3. Take small pieces of the dough and roll into balls. Place well apart on greased baking sheets and flatten slightly with a fork or palette knife.

4. Bake one tray at a time for 5-10 minutes in an oven preheated to 190°C/375°F/Gas Mark 5. Cool slightly on the tray then transfer to a wire rack to cool completely.

TIME: Preparation takes about 15 minutes, cooking time is about 10 minutes.

PREPARATION: If the biscuit dough is too soft, add a little extra flour.

Banana Loaf

Eat this on its own as a cake, or slice thinly and butter to serve for elevenses or afternoon tea.

MAKES 1 LOAF

1 tea cup of porridge oats
1 tea cup of sugar
1 tea cup of mixed fruit
1 tea cup of Granose banana-flavoured soya milk
1 breakfast cup of self-raising flour
Pinch of nutmeg

1. Begin preparing the cake the day before it is to be cooked. Place all the ingredients except the self-raising flour and nutmeg into a large bowl and stir well.

2. Cover and put into the refrigerator overnight.

3. The following day, line or grease a 460g/1lb loaf tin.

4. Mix the self-raising flour and the nutmeg gently into the mixture and put into the loaf tin.

5. Bake in an oven preheated to 180°C/350°F/ Gas Mark 4, for an hour or until a skewer inserted into the loaf comes out clean.

TIME: Preparation takes 10 minutes, cooking takes 1 hour.

VARIATIONS: ½ tsp of mixed spice may be used in place of the nutmeg. Ordinary milk or plain soya milk can be used instead of banana soya milk.

SERVING IDEA: Eat on its own as a cake, or slice thinly and butter to serve for elevenses or afternoon tea.

COOK'S TIP: The loaf becomes more moist if left in an airtight tin for a day or two before eating.

Cinnamon Almond Slices

The combination of cinnamon with almond works perfectly in these tempting slices.

2 eggs
120g/4oz sugar
2 tbsps iced water
90g/3oz flour
1 tsp cinnamon
Pinch of salt
½ tsp baking powder
90g/3oz flaked almonds
Caster sugar

1. Beat the eggs and sugar together until light and fluffy, then beat in the iced water.

2. Sift the flour, cinnamon, salt and baking powder into the egg mixture. Add the almonds and mix thoroughly.

3. Pour the mixture into a well-greased square cake tin. Sprinkle the top with sugar.

4. Bake in an oven preheated to 180°C/350°F/Gas Mark 4, for about 25 minutes. Allow to cool, then cut into slices.

TIME: Preparation takes about 15 minutes and cooking takes 25 minutes.

VARIATION: Substitute allspice and hazelnuts for a different flavour.

Gingerbread

Dark treacle and fresh ginger combine to make this favourite family cake.

MAKES ONE 17.5cm/7-inch SQUARE CAKE

120g/4oz unsalted butter
120ml/4 fl oz black treacle
225g/8oz light soft brown sugar
120ml/4 fl oz hot water
275g/10oz plain flour
2 tsps baking powder
2 tsps peeled and grated fresh root ginger
1 tsp grated nutmeg
1 egg, beaten

1. Put the butter into a large saucepan, along with the treacle and sugar. Heat gently, stirring all the time, until the sugar and butter have melted together.

2. Pour in the hot water, mix well and set aside.

3. Sift the flour with the baking powder into a large bowl. Make a well in the centre, and add the ginger, nutmeg and beaten egg.

4. Gradually beat in the treacle, using a wooden spoon, slowly drawing the flour from the outside into the centre.

5. Line the base of a 17.5cm/7-inch square cake tin with silicone or lightly greased greaseproof paper.

6. Pour the gingerbread mixture into the cake tin, and bake in a preheated oven at 160°C/325°F/Gas Mark 3, for 1-1½ hours. Test during this time with a skewer; it should come out clean when the cake is cooked.

7. Allow the cake to cool in the tin, before turning out onto a wire rack. Cut into squares to serve.

TIME: Preparation takes about 15 minutes, cooking takes 1-1½ hours.

VARIATION: Add 60g/2oz chopped mixed fruit to the gingerbread mixture along with the spices.

SERVING IDEA: Serve as a dessert with a lemon sauce.

TO FREEZE: This cake freezes well for up to 1 month.

Index